Congratulations on the birth c

We know this is probably not ＿＿＿＿＿＿＿＿ and you are currently going through the unimaginable but we hope you can find some comfort in knowing you are definitely not alone.

We are Lisa and Stacey two preemie mums who have experienced the NICU too.
Lisa had her son at 30 weeks and Stacey is a mum to a 32 weeker.

As preemie parents, we know just how crazy the NICU experience can be and how each day blurs into the next, which is why we created this diary for you to be able to document your journey each day and never forget your baby's story!

The beautiful duck, dinosaur and giraffe characters you see throughout this diary were created by the very talented Kerri Awosile. You will see sections to document all of your baby's milestones and memories. There is space to write your thoughts and a few full pages for you to stick your special photos so you can see the progress your baby is making.

We sincerely hope you find this diary a useful tool, not only throughout your neonatal stay but beyond the NICU too!

With love and hugs

Lisa and Stacey xxx

Presents for Preemies is not only a gifting service, we also have an established blog, sharing expertise and experiences from ourselves and guest experts. www.presentsforpreemies.co.uk/blog/
We also have our much loved group the Preemie Support Village on Facebook. Welcoming those affected by the birth of a premature baby.
www.facebook.com/groups/preemiesupportvillage/
You can also find us on Instagram
www.instagram.com/presents_for_preemies

PRESENTS FOR PREEMIES
Thoughtful gifts for early arrivals

When I Was Born

Birthday:

Time:

Gestation:

Weight:

Length:

My Midwife:

My Doctor:

My Neonatal Nurse:

Reason for Early Arrival:

Todays Date

ALL ABOUT ME!

DAY NUMBER _____ IN NICU

Gestational Age:

Weight:

Vital Signs:

WHO LOOKED AFTER ME TODAY?

PROGRESS MADE

BUMPS IN THE ROAD

WHAT DID WE DO TODAY?

MY GROWNS UP'S THOUGHTS!

FEEDING REGIME

HOW MUCH

HOW OFTEN

WHAT METHOD

FAMILY & FRIENDS FROM TODAY

QUESTIONS & THINGS TO REMEMBER

Todays Date

DAY NUMBER _____ IN NICU

Gestational Age:

Weight:

WHO LOOKED AFTER ME TODAY?

Vital Signs:

PROGRESS MADE

BUMPS IN THE ROAD

WHAT DID WE DO TODAY?

MY GROWNS UP'S THOUGHTS!

FEEDING REGIME

FAMILY & FRIENDS FROM TODAY

HOW MUCH

HOW OFTEN

WHAT METHOD

QUESTIONS & THINGS TO REMEMBER

Todays Date

DAY NUMBER _____ IN NICU

Gestational Age:

Weight:

Vital Signs:

WHO LOOKED AFTER ME TODAY?

PROGRESS MADE

BUMPS IN THE ROAD

WHAT DID WE DO TODAY?

MY GROWN'S UP'S THOUGHTS!

FEEDING REGIME

HOW MUCH

HOW OFTEN

WHAT METHOD

FAMILY & FRIENDS FROM TODAY

QUESTIONS & THINGS TO REMEMBER

Todays Date

DAY NUMBER _____ IN NICU

Gestational Age:

Weight:

WHO LOOKED AFTER ME TODAY?

Vital Signs:

PROGRESS MADE

BUMPS IN THE ROAD

WHAT DID WE DO TODAY?

MY GROWN'S UP'S THOUGHTS!

FEEDING REGIME

HOW MUCH

HOW OFTEN

WHAT METHOD

FAMILY & FRIENDS FROM TODAY

QUESTIONS & THINGS TO REMEMBER

Todays Date

DAY NUMBER _____ IN NICU

Gestational Age:

Weight:

Vital Signs:

WHO LOOKED AFTER ME TODAY?

PROGRESS MADE

BUMPS IN THE ROAD

WHAT DID WE DO TODAY?

MY GROWNS UP'S THOUGHTS!

FEEDING REGIME

HOW MUCH

HOW OFTEN

WHAT METHOD

FAMILY & FRIENDS FROM TODAY

QUESTIONS & THINGS TO REMEMBER

Todays Date

DAY NUMBER _____ IN NICU

Gestational Age:

Weight:

Vital Signs:

WHO LOOKED AFTER ME TODAY?

PROGRESS MADE

BUMPS IN THE ROAD

WHAT DID WE DO TODAY?

MY GROWNS UP'S THOUGHTS!

FEEDING REGIME

HOW MUCH

HOW OFTEN

WHAT METHOD

FAMILY & FRIENDS FROM TODAY

QUESTIONS & THINGS TO REMEMBER

Todays Date

ALL ABOUT ME!

DAY NUMBER _____ IN NICU

Gestational Age:

Weight:

Vital Signs:

WHO LOOKED AFTER ME TODAY?

PROGRESS MADE

BUMPS IN THE ROAD

WHAT DID WE DO TODAY?

FEEDING REGIME

HOW MUCH

HOW OFTEN

WHAT METHOD

FAMILY & FRIENDS FROM TODAY

QUESTIONS & THINGS TO REMEMBER

Todays Date

ALL ABOUT ME!

DAY NUMBER _____ IN NICU

Gestational Age:

Weight:

Vital Signs:

WHO LOOKED AFTER ME TODAY?

PROGRESS MADE

BUMPS IN THE ROAD

WHAT DID WE DO TODAY?

MY GROWNS UP'S THOUGHTS!

FEEDING REGIME

HOW MUCH

HOW OFTEN

WHAT METHOD

FAMILY & FRIENDS FROM TODAY

QUESTIONS & THINGS TO REMEMBER

Todays Date

DAY NUMBER _____ IN NICU

Gestational Age:

Weight:

WHO LOOKED AFTER ME TODAY?

Vital Signs:

PROGRESS MADE

BUMPS IN THE ROAD

WHAT DID WE DO TODAY?

MY GROWNS UP'S THOUGHTS!

FEEDING REGIME

HOW MUCH

HOW OFTEN

WHAT METHOD

FAMILY & FRIENDS FROM TODAY

QUESTIONS & THINGS TO REMEMBER

Todays Date

ALL ABOUT ME!

DAY NUMBER _____ IN NICU

Gestational Age:

Weight:

Vital Signs:

WHO LOOKED AFTER ME TODAY?

PROGRESS MADE

BUMPS IN THE ROAD

WHAT DID WE DO TODAY?

MY GROWNS UP'S THOUGHTS!

FEEDING REGIME

HOW MUCH

HOW OFTEN

WHAT METHOD

FAMILY & FRIENDS FROM TODAY

QUESTIONS & THINGS TO REMEMBER

Todays Date

ALL ABOUT ME!

DAY NUMBER _____ IN NICU

Gestational Age:

Weight:

Vital Signs:

WHO LOOKED AFTER ME TODAY?

PROGRESS MADE

BUMPS IN THE ROAD

WHAT DID WE DO TODAY?

MY GROWNS UP'S THOUGHTS!

FEEDING REGIME

HOW MUCH

HOW OFTEN

WHAT METHOD

FAMILY & FRIENDS FROM TODAY

QUESTIONS & THINGS TO REMEMBER

Todays Date

DAY NUMBER _____ IN NICU

Gestational Age:

Weight:

WHO LOOKED AFTER ME TODAY?

Vital Signs:

PROGRESS MADE

BUMPS IN THE ROAD

WHAT DID WE DO TODAY?

MY GROWNS UP'S THOUGHTS!

FEEDING REGIME

HOW MUCH

HOW OFTEN

WHAT METHOD

FAMILY & FRIENDS FROM TODAY

QUESTIONS & THINGS TO REMEMBER

Todays Date

DAY NUMBER _____ IN NICU

Gestational Age:

Weight:

WHO LOOKED AFTER ME TODAY?

Vital Signs:

PROGRESS MADE

BUMPS IN THE ROAD

WHAT DID WE DO TODAY?

MY GROWNS UP'S THOUGHTS!

FEEDING REGIME

FAMILY & FRIENDS FROM TODAY

HOW MUCH

HOW OFTEN

WHAT METHOD

QUESTIONS & THINGS TO REMEMBER

Todays Date

DAY NUMBER _____ IN NICU

WHO LOOKED AFTER ME TODAY?

Gestational Age:

Weight:

Vital Signs:

PROGRESS MADE

BUMPS IN THE ROAD

WHAT DID WE DO TODAY?

MY GROWNS UP'S THOUGHTS!

FEEDING REGIME

HOW MUCH

HOW OFTEN

WHAT METHOD

FAMILY & FRIENDS FROM TODAY

QUESTIONS & THINGS TO REMEMBER

Todays Date

DAY NUMBER _____ IN NICU

Gestational Age:

Weight:

WHO LOOKED AFTER ME TODAY?

Vital Signs:

PROGRESS MADE

BUMPS IN THE ROAD

WHAT DID WE DO TODAY?

MY GROWN'S UP'S THOUGHTS!

FEEDING REGIME

HOW MUCH

HOW OFTEN

WHAT METHOD

FAMILY & FRIENDS FROM TODAY

QUESTIONS & THINGS TO REMEMBER

Todays Date

ALL ABOUT ME!

DAY NUMBER _____ IN NICU

Gestational Age:

Weight:

Vital Signs:

WHO LOOKED AFTER ME TODAY?

PROGRESS MADE

BUMPS IN THE ROAD

WHAT DID WE DO TODAY?

MY GROWNS UP'S THOUGHTS!

FEEDING REGIME

FAMILY & FRIENDS FROM TODAY

HOW MUCH

HOW OFTEN

WHAT METHOD

QUESTIONS & THINGS TO REMEMBER

Todays Date

ALL ABOUT ME!

DAY NUMBER _____ IN NICU

Gestational Age:

Weight:

Vital Signs:

WHO LOOKED AFTER ME TODAY?

PROGRESS MADE

BUMPS IN THE ROAD

WHAT DID WE DO TODAY?

MY GROWNS UP'S THOUGHTS!

FEEDING REGIME

HOW MUCH

HOW OFTEN

WHAT METHOD

FAMILY & FRIENDS FROM TODAY

QUESTIONS & THINGS TO REMEMBER

Todays Date

DAY NUMBER _____ IN NICU

Gestational Age:

Weight:

WHO LOOKED AFTER ME TODAY?

Vital Signs:

PROGRESS MADE

BUMPS IN THE ROAD

WHAT DID WE DO TODAY?

MY GROWNS UP'S THOUGHTS!

FEEDING REGIME

HOW MUCH

HOW OFTEN

WHAT METHOD

FAMILY & FRIENDS FROM TODAY

QUESTIONS & THINGS TO REMEMBER

Todays Date

DAY NUMBER _____ IN NICU

Gestational Age:

Weight:

Vital Signs:

WHO LOOKED AFTER ME TODAY?

PROGRESS MADE

BUMPS IN THE ROAD

WHAT DID WE DO TODAY?

MY GROWN'S UP'S THOUGHTS!

FEEDING REGIME

HOW MUCH

HOW OFTEN

WHAT METHOD

FAMILY & FRIENDS FROM TODAY

QUESTIONS & THINGS TO REMEMBER

Todays Date

DAY NUMBER _____ IN NICU

Gestational Age:

Weight:

Vital Signs:

WHO LOOKED AFTER ME TODAY?

PROGRESS MADE

BUMPS IN THE ROAD

WHAT DID WE DO TODAY?

MY GROWNS UP'S THOUGHTS!

FEEDING REGIME

HOW MUCH

HOW OFTEN

WHAT METHOD

FAMILY & FRIENDS FROM TODAY

QUESTIONS & THINGS TO REMEMBER

Todays Date

DAY NUMBER _____ IN NICU

Gestational Age:

Weight:

WHO LOOKED AFTER ME TODAY?

Vital Signs:

PROGRESS MADE

BUMPS IN THE ROAD

WHAT DID WE DO TODAY?

MY GROWNS UP'S THOUGHTS!

FEEDING REGIME

HOW MUCH

HOW OFTEN

WHAT METHOD

FAMILY & FRIENDS FROM TODAY

QUESTIONS & THINGS TO REMEMBER

Todays Date

DAY NUMBER _____ IN NICU

Gestational Age:

Weight:

Vital Signs:

WHO LOOKED AFTER ME TODAY?

PROGRESS MADE

BUMPS IN THE ROAD

WHAT DID WE DO TODAY?

FEEDING REGIME

FAMILY & FRIENDS FROM TODAY

HOW MUCH

HOW OFTEN

WHAT METHOD

QUESTIONS & THINGS TO REMEMBER

Todays Date

DAY NUMBER _____ IN NICU

Gestational Age:

Weight:

WHO LOOKED AFTER ME TODAY?

Vital Signs:

PROGRESS MADE

BUMPS IN THE ROAD

WHAT DID WE DO TODAY?

MY GROWN'S UP'S THOUGHTS!

FEEDING REGIME

HOW MUCH

HOW OFTEN

WHAT METHOD

FAMILY & FRIENDS FROM TODAY

QUESTIONS & THINGS TO REMEMBER

Todays Date

ALL ABOUT ME!

DAY NUMBER _____ IN NICU

Gestational Age:

Weight:

WHO LOOKED AFTER ME TODAY?

Vital Signs:

PROGRESS MADE

BUMPS IN THE ROAD

WHAT DID WE DO TODAY?

MY GROWNS UP'S THOUGHTS!

FEEDING REGIME

HOW MUCH

HOW OFTEN

WHAT METHOD

FAMILY & FRIENDS FROM TODAY

QUESTIONS & THINGS TO REMEMBER

Todays Date

ALL ABOUT ME!

DAY NUMBER _____ IN NICU

Gestational Age:

Weight:

Vital Signs:

WHO LOOKED AFTER ME TODAY?

PROGRESS MADE

BUMPS IN THE ROAD

WHAT DID WE DO TODAY?

MY GROWNS UP'S THOUGHTS!

FEEDING REGIME

HOW MUCH

HOW OFTEN

WHAT METHOD

FAMILY & FRIENDS FROM TODAY

QUESTIONS & THINGS TO REMEMBER

Todays Date

DAY NUMBER _____ IN NICU

Gestational Age:

Weight:

Vital Signs:

WHO LOOKED AFTER ME TODAY?

PROGRESS MADE

BUMPS IN THE ROAD

WHAT DID WE DO TODAY?

MY GROWN'S UP'S THOUGHTS!

FEEDING REGIME

HOW MUCH

HOW OFTEN

WHAT METHOD

FAMILY & FRIENDS FROM TODAY

QUESTIONS & THINGS TO REMEMBER

Todays Date

DAY NUMBER _____ IN NICU

Gestational Age:

Weight:

WHO LOOKED AFTER ME TODAY?

Vital Signs:

PROGRESS MADE

BUMPS IN THE ROAD

WHAT DID WE DO TODAY?

MY GROWNS UP'S THOUGHTS!

FEEDING REGIME

HOW MUCH

HOW OFTEN

WHAT METHOD

FAMILY & FRIENDS FROM TODAY

QUESTIONS & THINGS TO REMEMBER

Todays Date

ALL ABOUT ME!

DAY NUMBER _____ IN NICU

Gestational Age:

Weight:

Vital Signs:

WHO LOOKED AFTER ME TODAY?

PROGRESS MADE

BUMPS IN THE ROAD

WHAT DID WE DO TODAY?

MY GROWNS UP'S THOUGHTS!

FEEDING REGIME

HOW MUCH

HOW OFTEN

WHAT METHOD

FAMILY & FRIENDS FROM TODAY

QUESTIONS & THINGS TO REMEMBER

Todays Date

DAY NUMBER _____ IN NICU

Gestational Age:

Weight:

Vital Signs:

WHO LOOKED AFTER ME TODAY?

PROGRESS MADE

BUMPS IN THE ROAD

WHAT DID WE DO TODAY?

FEEDING REGIME

HOW MUCH

HOW OFTEN

WHAT METHOD

FAMILY & FRIENDS FROM TODAY

QUESTIONS & THINGS TO REMEMBER

Todays Date

DAY NUMBER _____ IN NICU

Gestational Age:

Weight:

WHO LOOKED AFTER ME TODAY?

Vital Signs:

PROGRESS MADE

BUMPS IN THE ROAD

WHAT DID WE DO TODAY?

MY GROWN'S UP'S THOUGHTS!

FEEDING REGIME

HOW MUCH

HOW OFTEN

WHAT METHOD

FAMILY & FRIENDS FROM TODAY

QUESTIONS & THINGS TO REMEMBER

Todays Date

DAY NUMBER _____ IN NICU

Gestational Age:

Weight:

Vital Signs:

WHO LOOKED AFTER ME TODAY?

PROGRESS MADE

BUMPS IN THE ROAD

WHAT DID WE DO TODAY?

MY GROWN5 UP'S THOUGHTS!

FEEDING REGIME

FAMILY & FRIENDS FROM TODAY

HOW MUCH

HOW OFTEN

WHAT METHOD

QUESTIONS & THINGS TO REMEMBER

Todays Date

DAY NUMBER _____ IN NICU

Gestational Age:

Weight:

Vital Signs:

WHO LOOKED AFTER ME TODAY?

PROGRESS MADE

BUMPS IN THE ROAD

WHAT DID WE DO TODAY?

MY GROWNS UP'S THOUGHTS!

FEEDING REGIME

HOW MUCH

HOW OFTEN

WHAT METHOD

FAMILY & FRIENDS FROM TODAY

QUESTIONS & THINGS TO REMEMBER

Todays Date

DAY NUMBER _____ IN NICU

Gestational Age:

Weight:

WHO LOOKED AFTER ME TODAY?

Vital Signs:

PROGRESS MADE

BUMPS IN THE ROAD

WHAT DID WE DO TODAY?

MY GROWNS UP'S THOUGHTS!

FEEDING REGIME

HOW MUCH

HOW OFTEN

WHAT METHOD

FAMILY & FRIENDS FROM TODAY

QUESTIONS & THINGS TO REMEMBER

Todays Date

DAY NUMBER _____ IN NICU

Gestational Age:

Weight:

WHO LOOKED AFTER ME TODAY?

Vital Signs:

PROGRESS MADE

BUMPS IN THE ROAD

WHAT DID WE DO TODAY?

FEEDING REGIME

HOW MUCH

HOW OFTEN

WHAT METHOD

FAMILY & FRIENDS FROM TODAY

QUESTIONS & THINGS TO REMEMBER

Todays Date

DAY NUMBER _____ IN NICU

Gestational Age:

Weight:

Vital Signs:

WHO LOOKED AFTER ME TODAY?

PROGRESS MADE

BUMPS IN THE ROAD

WHAT DID WE DO TODAY?

FEEDING REGIME

HOW MUCH

HOW OFTEN

WHAT METHOD

FAMILY & FRIENDS FROM TODAY

QUESTIONS & THINGS TO REMEMBER

Todays Date

DAY NUMBER _____ IN NICU

Gestational Age:

Weight:

Vital Signs:

WHO LOOKED AFTER ME TODAY?

PROGRESS MADE

BUMPS IN THE ROAD

WHAT DID WE DO TODAY?

MY GROWNS UP'S THOUGHTS!

FEEDING REGIME

HOW MUCH

HOW OFTEN

WHAT METHOD

FAMILY & FRIENDS FROM TODAY

QUESTIONS & THINGS TO REMEMBER

Todays Date

DAY NUMBER _____ IN NICU

Gestational Age:

Weight:

Vital Signs:

WHO LOOKED AFTER ME TODAY?

PROGRESS MADE

BUMPS IN THE ROAD

WHAT DID WE DO TODAY?

FEEDING REGIME

FAMILY & FRIENDS FROM TODAY

HOW MUCH

HOW OFTEN

WHAT METHOD

QUESTIONS & THINGS TO REMEMBER

Todays Date

ALL ABOUT ME!

DAY NUMBER _____ IN NICU

Gestational Age:

Weight:

WHO LOOKED AFTER ME TODAY?

Vital Signs:

PROGRESS MADE

BUMPS IN THE ROAD

WHAT DID WE DO TODAY?

MY GROWN'S UP'S THOUGHTS!

FEEDING REGIME

HOW MUCH

HOW OFTEN

WHAT METHOD

FAMILY & FRIENDS FROM TODAY

QUESTIONS & THINGS TO REMEMBER

Todays Date

ALL ABOUT ME!

DAY NUMBER _____ IN NICU

Gestational Age:

Weight:

Vital Signs:

WHO LOOKED AFTER ME TODAY?

PROGRESS MADE

BUMPS IN THE ROAD

WHAT DID WE DO TODAY?

MY GROWNS UP'S THOUGHTS!

FEEDING REGIME

HOW MUCH

HOW OFTEN

WHAT METHOD

FAMILY & FRIENDS FROM TODAY

QUESTIONS & THINGS TO REMEMBER

Todays Date

ALL ABOUT ME!

DAY NUMBER _____ IN NICU

Gestational Age:

Weight:

WHO LOOKED AFTER ME TODAY?

Vital Signs:

PROGRESS MADE

BUMPS IN THE ROAD

WHAT DID WE DO TODAY?

FEEDING REGIME

HOW MUCH

HOW OFTEN

WHAT METHOD

FAMILY & FRIENDS FROM TODAY

QUESTIONS & THINGS TO REMEMBER

Todays Date

DAY NUMBER _____ IN NICU

Gestational Age:

Weight:

WHO LOOKED AFTER ME TODAY?

Vital Signs:

PROGRESS MADE

BUMPS IN THE ROAD

WHAT DID WE DO TODAY?

MY GROWN'S UP'S THOUGHTS!

FEEDING REGIME

HOW MUCH

HOW OFTEN

WHAT METHOD

FAMILY & FRIENDS FROM TODAY

QUESTIONS & THINGS TO REMEMBER

Todays Date

DAY NUMBER _____ IN NICU

Gestational Age:

Weight:

Vital Signs:

WHO LOOKED AFTER ME TODAY?

PROGRESS MADE

BUMPS IN THE ROAD

WHAT DID WE DO TODAY?

MY GROWNS UP'S THOUGHTS!

FEEDING REGIME

HOW MUCH

HOW OFTEN

WHAT METHOD

FAMILY & FRIENDS FROM TODAY

QUESTIONS & THINGS TO REMEMBER

Todays Date

DAY NUMBER _____ IN NICU

Gestational Age:

Weight:

WHO LOOKED AFTER ME TODAY?

Vital Signs:

PROGRESS MADE

BUMPS IN THE ROAD

WHAT DID WE DO TODAY?

FEEDING REGIME

HOW MUCH

HOW OFTEN

WHAT METHOD

FAMILY & FRIENDS FROM TODAY

QUESTIONS & THINGS TO REMEMBER

Todays Date

ALL ABOUT ME!

DAY NUMBER _____ IN NICU

Gestational Age:

Weight:

Vital Signs:

WHO LOOKED AFTER ME TODAY?

PROGRESS MADE

BUMPS IN THE ROAD

WHAT DID WE DO TODAY?

MY GROWNS UP'S THOUGHTS!

FEEDING REGIME

HOW MUCH

HOW OFTEN

WHAT METHOD

FAMILY & FRIENDS FROM TODAY

QUESTIONS & THINGS TO REMEMBER

Todays Date

DAY NUMBER _____ IN NICU

Gestational Age:

Weight:

WHO LOOKED AFTER ME TODAY?

Vital Signs:

PROGRESS MADE

BUMPS IN THE ROAD

WHAT DID WE DO TODAY?

MY GROWNS UP'S THOUGHTS!

FEEDING REGIME

HOW MUCH

HOW OFTEN

WHAT METHOD

FAMILY & FRIENDS FROM TODAY

QUESTIONS & THINGS TO REMEMBER

Todays Date

ALL ABOUT ME!

DAY NUMBER _____ IN NICU

Gestational Age:

Weight:

WHO LOOKED AFTER ME TODAY?

Vital Signs:

PROGRESS MADE

BUMPS IN THE ROAD

WHAT DID WE DO TODAY?

MY GROWNS UP'S THOUGHTS!

FEEDING REGIME

FAMILY & FRIENDS FROM TODAY

HOW MUCH

HOW OFTEN

WHAT METHOD

QUESTIONS & THINGS TO REMEMBER

Todays Date

ALL ABOUT ME!

DAY NUMBER _____ IN NICU

Gestational Age:

Weight:

Vital Signs:

WHO LOOKED AFTER ME TODAY?

PROGRESS MADE

BUMPS IN THE ROAD

WHAT DID WE DO TODAY?

MY GROWN'S UP'S THOUGHTS!

FEEDING REGIME

HOW MUCH

HOW OFTEN

WHAT METHOD

FAMILY & FRIENDS FROM TODAY

QUESTIONS & THINGS TO REMEMBER

Todays Date

DAY NUMBER _____ IN NICU

Gestational Age:

Weight:

WHO LOOKED AFTER ME TODAY?

Vital Signs:

PROGRESS MADE

BUMPS IN THE ROAD

WHAT DID WE DO TODAY?

FEEDING REGIME

HOW MUCH

HOW OFTEN

WHAT METHOD

FAMILY & FRIENDS FROM TODAY

QUESTIONS & THINGS TO REMEMBER

Todays Date

DAY NUMBER _____ IN NICU

Gestational Age:

Weight:

WHO LOOKED AFTER ME TODAY?

Vital Signs:

PROGRESS MADE

BUMPS IN THE ROAD

WHAT DID WE DO TODAY?

MY GROWNS UP'S THOUGHTS!

FEEDING REGIME

FAMILY & FRIENDS FROM TODAY

HOW MUCH

HOW OFTEN

WHAT METHOD

QUESTIONS & THINGS TO REMEMBER

Todays Date

DAY NUMBER _____ IN NICU

Gestational Age:

Weight:

Vital Signs:

WHO LOOKED AFTER ME TODAY?

PROGRESS MADE

BUMPS IN THE ROAD

WHAT DID WE DO TODAY?

MY GROWNS UP'S THOUGHTS!

FEEDING REGIME

HOW MUCH

HOW OFTEN

WHAT METHOD

FAMILY & FRIENDS FROM TODAY

QUESTIONS & THINGS TO REMEMBER

Todays Date

DAY NUMBER _____ IN NICU

Gestational Age:

Weight:

WHO LOOKED AFTER ME TODAY?

Vital Signs:

PROGRESS MADE

BUMPS IN THE ROAD

WHAT DID WE DO TODAY?

MY GROWNS UP'S THOUGHTS!

FEEDING REGIME

HOW MUCH

HOW OFTEN

WHAT METHOD

FAMILY & FRIENDS FROM TODAY

QUESTIONS & THINGS TO REMEMBER

Todays Date

ALL ABOUT ME!

DAY NUMBER _____ IN NICU

Gestational Age:

Weight:

Vital Signs:

WHO LOOKED AFTER ME TODAY?

PROGRESS MADE

BUMPS IN THE ROAD

WHAT DID WE DO TODAY?

MY GROWNS UP'S THOUGHTS!

FEEDING REGIME

HOW MUCH

HOW OFTEN

WHAT METHOD

FAMILY & FRIENDS FROM TODAY

QUESTIONS & THINGS TO REMEMBER

Todays Date

DAY NUMBER _____ IN NICU

Gestational Age:

Weight:

WHO LOOKED AFTER ME TODAY?

Vital Signs:

PROGRESS MADE

BUMPS IN THE ROAD

WHAT DID WE DO TODAY?

MY GROWN'S UP'S THOUGHTS!

FEEDING REGIME

HOW MUCH

HOW OFTEN

WHAT METHOD

FAMILY & FRIENDS FROM TODAY

QUESTIONS & THINGS TO REMEMBER

Todays Date

DAY NUMBER _____ IN NICU

Gestational Age:

Weight:

WHO LOOKED AFTER ME TODAY?

Vital Signs:

PROGRESS MADE

BUMPS IN THE ROAD

WHAT DID WE DO TODAY?

MY GROWNS UP'S THOUGHTS!

FEEDING REGIME

HOW MUCH

HOW OFTEN

WHAT METHOD

FAMILY & FRIENDS FROM TODAY

QUESTIONS & THINGS TO REMEMBER

Todays Date

DAY NUMBER _____ IN NICU

Gestational Age:

Weight:

Vital Signs:

WHO LOOKED AFTER ME TODAY?

PROGRESS MADE

BUMPS IN THE ROAD

WHAT DID WE DO TODAY?

MY GROWNS UP'S THOUGHTS!

FEEDING REGIME

HOW MUCH

HOW OFTEN

WHAT METHOD

FAMILY & FRIENDS FROM TODAY

QUESTIONS & THINGS TO REMEMBER

Todays Date

DAY NUMBER _____ IN NICU

Gestational Age:

Weight:

Vital Signs:

WHO LOOKED AFTER ME TODAY?

PROGRESS MADE

BUMPS IN THE ROAD

WHAT DID WE DO TODAY?

MY GROWNS UP'S THOUGHTS!

FEEDING REGIME

HOW MUCH

HOW OFTEN

WHAT METHOD

FAMILY & FRIENDS FROM TODAY

QUESTIONS & THINGS TO REMEMBER

Todays Date

DAY NUMBER _____ IN NICU

Gestational Age:

Weight:

WHO LOOKED AFTER ME TODAY?

Vital Signs:

PROGRESS MADE

BUMPS IN THE ROAD

WHAT DID WE DO TODAY?

MY GROWNS UP'S THOUGHTS!

FEEDING REGIME

HOW MUCH

HOW OFTEN

WHAT METHOD

FAMILY & FRIENDS FROM TODAY

QUESTIONS & THINGS TO REMEMBER

Todays Date

ALL ABOUT ME!

DAY NUMBER _____ IN NICU

Gestational Age:

Weight:

WHO LOOKED AFTER ME TODAY?

Vital Signs:

PROGRESS MADE

BUMPS IN THE ROAD

WHAT DID WE DO TODAY?

MY GROWNS UP'S THOUGHTS!

FEEDING REGIME

HOW MUCH

HOW OFTEN

WHAT METHOD

FAMILY & FRIENDS FROM TODAY

QUESTIONS & THINGS TO REMEMBER

Todays Date

ALL ABOUT ME!

DAY NUMBER _____ IN NICU

Gestational Age:

Weight:

Vital Signs:

WHO LOOKED AFTER ME TODAY?

PROGRESS MADE

BUMPS IN THE ROAD

WHAT DID WE DO TODAY?

MY GROWNS UP'S THOUGHTS!

FEEDING REGIME

HOW MUCH

HOW OFTEN

WHAT METHOD

FAMILY & FRIENDS FROM TODAY

QUESTIONS & THINGS TO REMEMBER

Todays Date

ALL ABOUT ME!

DAY NUMBER _____ IN NICU

Gestational Age:

Weight:

WHO LOOKED AFTER ME TODAY?

Vital Signs:

PROGRESS MADE

BUMPS IN THE ROAD

WHAT DID WE DO TODAY?

MY GROWN'S UP'S THOUGHTS!

FEEDING REGIME

HOW MUCH

HOW OFTEN

WHAT METHOD

FAMILY & FRIENDS FROM TODAY

QUESTIONS & THINGS TO REMEMBER

Todays Date

DAY NUMBER _____ IN NICU

Gestational Age:

Weight:

WHO LOOKED AFTER ME TODAY?

Vital Signs:

PROGRESS MADE

BUMPS IN THE ROAD

WHAT DID WE DO TODAY?

MY GROWNS UP'S THOUGHTS!

FEEDING REGIME

HOW MUCH

HOW OFTEN

WHAT METHOD

FAMILY & FRIENDS FROM TODAY

QUESTIONS & THINGS TO REMEMBER

Todays Date

DAY NUMBER _____ IN NICU

Gestational Age:

Weight:

WHO LOOKED AFTER ME TODAY?

Vital Signs:

PROGRESS MADE

BUMPS IN THE ROAD

WHAT DID WE DO TODAY?

MY GROWNS UP'S THOUGHTS!

FEEDING REGIME

HOW MUCH

HOW OFTEN

WHAT METHOD

FAMILY & FRIENDS FROM TODAY

QUESTIONS & THINGS TO REMEMBER

Todays Date

ALL ABOUT ME!

DAY NUMBER _____ IN NICU

Gestational Age:

Weight:

WHO LOOKED AFTER ME TODAY?

Vital Signs:

PROGRESS MADE

BUMPS IN THE ROAD

WHAT DID WE DO TODAY?

MY GROWN'S UP'S THOUGHTS!

FEEDING REGIME

HOW MUCH

HOW OFTEN

WHAT METHOD

FAMILY & FRIENDS FROM TODAY

QUESTIONS & THINGS TO REMEMBER

Todays Date

ALL ABOUT ME!

DAY NUMBER _____ IN NICU

Gestational Age:

Weight:

Vital Signs:

WHO LOOKED AFTER ME TODAY?

PROGRESS MADE

BUMPS IN THE ROAD

WHAT DID WE DO TODAY?

MY GROWNS UP'S THOUGHTS!

FEEDING REGIME

FAMILY & FRIENDS FROM TODAY

HOW MUCH

HOW OFTEN

WHAT METHOD

QUESTIONS & THINGS TO REMEMBER

NOTES

QUOTE / SAYING OF THE DAY

QUOTE / SAYING OF THE DAY

QUOTE / SAYING OF THE DAY

NOTES

QUOTE / SAYING OF THE DAY

QUOTE / SAYING OF THE DAY

QUOTE / SAYING OF THE DAY

Going Home

Date:

Days in NICU:

Time Leaving:

Gestational Age:

Actual Age:

Weight:

Length:

My Doctor:

My Discharge Nurse:

Who I'm going home with:

Medication Chart

MEDICATION & DOSE	M	T	W	TH	F	S	SU

Medication Chart

MEDICATION & DOSE	M	T	W	TH	F	S	SU

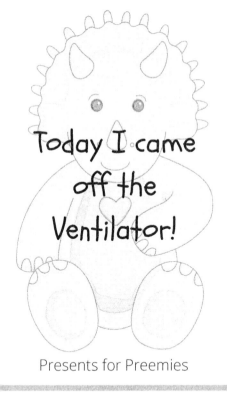

Today I came off the Ventilator!

Presents for Preemies

I'm now breathing Unaided!

Presents for Preemies

First Cuddle with Mum!

Presents for Preemies

First Cuddle with Dad!

Presents for Preemies

I moved to a crib today!

Presents for Preemies

Today I went Wireless!

Presents for Preemies

My First Feed! (without tubes)

Presents for Preemies

Today I wore my FIRST Outfit!

Presents for Preemies

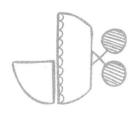

CONGRATULATIONS

This Certificate is presented to:

....

to celebrate your graduation from the NICU on ....

After........... days! You Are Amazing!! Enjoy being home with your family!

Presents for Preemies

Printed in Great Britain
by Amazon